EMMANUEL JOSEPH

Blockchain Bazaar: Mastering Crypto Exchange

Copyright © 2025 by Emmanuel Joseph

All rights reserved. No part of this publication may be reproduced, stored or transmitted in any form or by any means, electronic, mechanical, photocopying, recording, scanning, or otherwise without written permission from the publisher. It is illegal to copy this book, post it to a website, or distribute it by any other means without permission.

First edition

This book was professionally typeset on Reedsy.
Find out more at reedsy.com

Contents

1	Chapter 1: The Genesis of Blockchain	1
2	Chapter 2: Enter the Cryptocurrency Era	3
3	Chapter 3: The Anatomy of a Crypto Exchange	5
4	Chapter 4: Setting Up Your Exchange Account	7
5	Chapter 5: Navigating the Trading Interface	9
6	Chapter 6: Fundamental Analysis in Crypto Trading	11
7	Chapter 7: Technical Analysis in Crypto Trading	13
8	Chapter 8: Mastering Order Types and Strategies	15
9	Chapter 9: Risk Management and Trading Psychology	17
10	Chapter 10: Regulatory Landscape and Compliance	19
11	Chapter 11: Security Best Practices	21
12	Chapter 12: The Future of Crypto Exchanges	23

1

Chapter 1: The Genesis of Blockchain

Blockchain technology, the bedrock of cryptocurrency, has revolutionized digital transactions. Born from the need for a secure, decentralized method of recording transactions, it combines cryptographic principles with a decentralized ledger system. In the early days, few could predict its meteoric rise. Today, blockchain is not just a buzzword but a pillar of digital finance and beyond.

The concept first emerged with the advent of Bitcoin in 2009, introduced by the enigmatic Satoshi Nakamoto. Blockchain's primary appeal was its resistance to tampering and fraud, thanks to its decentralized nature. Each block in the chain contains a cryptographic hash of the previous block, ensuring the integrity of the entire chain. This breakthrough laid the foundation for all future cryptocurrencies.

Beyond Bitcoin, blockchain's potential applications became apparent. From supply chain management to voting systems, its decentralized and transparent nature offered solutions to age-old problems. As industries began to explore these possibilities, blockchain's versatility and robustness were put to the test, proving it could handle more than just digital currency transactions.

Today, blockchain is at the forefront of technological innovation. It's no longer confined to the realm of cryptocurrency but has found applications in healthcare, finance, and even entertainment. Its ability to provide secure, transparent, and efficient solutions makes it a technology with the potential to reshape entire industries.

2

Chapter 2: Enter the Cryptocurrency Era

Cryptocurrency, powered by blockchain technology, introduced a new paradigm in financial transactions. The decentralized nature of these digital currencies meant that traditional intermediaries like banks were no longer necessary. This shift promised lower transaction fees, faster transfers, and greater financial inclusion.

Bitcoin was the first and remains the most well-known cryptocurrency. However, its success paved the way for countless others, each with unique features and purposes. Ethereum, for instance, introduced smart contracts, enabling automated, self-executing agreements without the need for intermediaries. These innovations sparked a wave of creativity, leading to the development of thousands of cryptocurrencies.

The rise of cryptocurrencies also led to the creation of cryptocurrency exchanges. These platforms allowed users to buy, sell, and trade digital currencies, much like stock exchanges. However, they also faced unique challenges, such as security breaches and regulatory scrutiny. As a result, the industry quickly learned the importance of robust security measures and compliance with legal frameworks.

Despite the challenges, the cryptocurrency market has continued to grow. It's attracted a diverse range of investors, from tech-savvy early adopters to institutional investors seeking high returns. While the market remains volatile, the potential for significant gains keeps it an attractive option for many.

3

Chapter 3: The Anatomy of a Crypto Exchange

A cryptocurrency exchange is a platform where users can trade digital currencies. These exchanges come in various forms, each with its own set of features and benefits. Some are centralized, operated by a single entity, while others are decentralized, allowing users to trade directly with one another without intermediaries.

Centralized exchanges (CEXs) are the most common and are known for their user-friendly interfaces and high liquidity. They act as intermediaries, matching buyers and sellers and facilitating transactions. While they offer convenience and a wide range of trading pairs, they are also more vulnerable to hacking and regulatory oversight.

Decentralized exchanges (DEXs), on the other hand, operate without a central authority. They use smart contracts to automate transactions, providing users with greater control over their funds. DEXs are often lauded for their security and privacy, but they can be less intuitive for beginners and may suffer from lower liquidity compared to their centralized counterparts.

Hybrid exchanges aim to combine the best of both worlds, offering the security and control of a DEX with the user-friendly interface and liquidity of a CEX. These platforms are still relatively new but are gaining traction as they address the limitations of both centralized and decentralized exchanges.

Understanding the anatomy of a crypto exchange is crucial for anyone looking to trade digital currencies. Each type of exchange has its pros and cons, and choosing the right one depends on individual preferences and needs. Whether you prioritize security, liquidity, or ease of use, there's an exchange out there to suit your requirements.

4

Chapter 4: Setting Up Your Exchange Account

Creating an account on a cryptocurrency exchange is the first step towards engaging in digital currency trading. The process typically begins with selecting a reputable exchange that meets your needs. Factors to consider include security features, available trading pairs, fees, and user reviews.

Once you've chosen an exchange, you'll need to register an account. This usually involves providing an email address, creating a password, and verifying your identity. The identity verification process, known as KYC (Know Your Customer), is a standard procedure to prevent fraud and comply with regulatory requirements. It may require you to submit a government-issued ID and proof of address.

After successfully registering and verifying your account, the next step is to secure it. Enabling two-factor authentication (2FA) adds an extra layer of security by requiring a second form of verification, such as a code sent to your phone, whenever you log in or make a transaction. It's also important to use a strong, unique password and avoid sharing it with anyone.

With your account set up and secured, you're ready to deposit funds and start trading. Most exchanges support a variety of payment methods, including bank transfers, credit cards, and even other cryptocurrencies. Once your funds are deposited, you can begin exploring the available trading pairs and executing trades. Remember to start small and gradually increase your exposure as you become more comfortable with the platform.

5

Chapter 5: Navigating the Trading Interface

The trading interface of a cryptocurrency exchange can initially seem intimidating, especially for newcomers. However, understanding its key components and functions is essential for effective trading. Most exchanges offer similar features, including order books, trading charts, and various order types.

The order book is a real-time list of buy and sell orders on the exchange. It displays the prices and quantities of orders placed by other users, providing insight into market supply and demand. The order book is typically divided into two sections: the bid side (buy orders) and the ask side (sell orders).

Trading charts are visual representations of price movements over time. They provide valuable information for technical analysis, helping traders identify trends, support and resistance levels, and potential entry and exit points. Common chart types include line charts, bar charts, and candlestick charts, with candlesticks being the most popular among cryptocurrency traders.

Understanding different order types is crucial for executing trades effectively. The most basic order types are market orders and limit orders. A market order is executed immediately at the current market price, while a limit order is executed only when the price reaches a specified level. More advanced order types, such as stop-loss and take-profit orders, help manage risk and secure profits.

Familiarizing yourself with the trading interface and its features takes time and practice. Many exchanges offer demo accounts or paper trading options, allowing users to practice trading with virtual funds. Taking advantage of these tools can help you build confidence and refine your trading strategies before committing real money.

6

Chapter 6: Fundamental Analysis in Crypto Trading

Fundamental analysis is a method of evaluating the intrinsic value of an asset by examining various factors that could influence its price. In the context of cryptocurrency trading, fundamental analysis involves assessing the underlying technology, team, use cases, and market conditions of a digital asset.

One of the key aspects of fundamental analysis is understanding the technology behind a cryptocurrency. This includes evaluating the blockchain's consensus mechanism, scalability, security features, and potential for future development. A robust and innovative technology can provide a strong foundation for a cryptocurrency's long-term success.

The team behind a cryptocurrency project is another critical factor. Experienced and reputable developers, advisors, and partnerships can significantly impact a project's credibility and potential for success. Researching the team's background, track record, and vision can provide valuable insights into the project's prospects.

Analyzing the use cases and real-world applications of a cryptocurrency is also essential. A digital asset with practical use cases and widespread adoption is more likely to maintain and increase its value over time. Consider factors such as the target market, potential competitors, and the project's ability to solve real-world problems.

Finally, market conditions play a crucial role in fundamental analysis. This includes evaluating market sentiment, regulatory developments, and macroeconomic factors that could influence the cryptocurrency market. By considering these factors, traders can make more informed decisions and identify undervalued assets with growth potential.

7

Chapter 7: Technical Analysis in Crypto Trading

Technical analysis is a method of forecasting price movements by analyzing historical price data and trading volume. It involves using various tools and indicators to identify patterns, trends, and potential entry and exit points. Technical analysis is widely used in cryptocurrency trading due to the market's volatility and rapid price fluctuations.

One of the fundamental concepts in technical analysis is the identification of trends. Trends can be upward (bullish), downward (bearish), or sideways (neutral). Recognizing the direction of a trend helps traders align their strategies with the market's momentum. Trendlines, moving averages, and the Relative Strength Index (RSI) are common tools used to identify trends.

Support and resistance levels are critical components of technical analysis. Support levels are price points where an asset tends to find buying interest, preventing it from falling further. Resistance levels are price points where selling pressure tends to emerge, preventing the asset from rising further. Identifying these levels helps traders anticipate potential price reversals and set appropriate entry and exit points.

Technical indicators are mathematical calculations based on price and volume data. They help traders identify potential buy or sell signals and confirm trends. Some popular indicators include the Moving Average Convergence Divergence (MACD), Bollinger Bands, and the Fibonacci retracement. Each indicator has its strengths and weaknesses, and combining multiple indicators can provide a more comprehensive analysis.

Chart patterns are another crucial aspect of technical analysis. Patterns such as head and shoulders, double tops and bottoms, and triangles can indicate potential trend reversals or continuations. Recognizing these patterns and understanding their implications can help traders make more informed decisions and capitalize on market opportunities.

8

Chapter 8: Mastering Order Types and Strategies

Order types and trading strategies are fundamental aspects of successful cryptocurrency trading. Understanding the various order types and how to use them effectively can help traders manage risk and maximize profits. Additionally, developing and implementing trading strategies can provide a structured approach to navigating the volatile crypto market.

Market orders and limit orders are the most basic order types. A market order is executed immediately at the current market price, making it ideal for traders who want to quickly enter or exit a position. However, the price at which the order is executed may differ from the expected price due to market fluctuations. In contrast, a limit order is executed only when the price reaches a specified level, allowing traders to control the entry or exit price. While limit orders offer more precision, they may not be filled if the market price does not reach the specified level.

Stop orders are another essential order type used to manage risk. A stop-loss order is placed to sell a cryptocurrency when its price falls to a predetermined level, helping to minimize potential losses. Conversely, a take-profit order is placed to sell a cryptocurrency when its price rises to a predetermined level, securing profits. These orders can be particularly useful in volatile markets, where prices can change rapidly.

Trading strategies are systematic approaches to buying and selling cryptocurrencies based on predefined rules and criteria. Common strategies include day trading, swing trading, and long-term investing. Day trading involves making multiple trades within a single day to capitalize on short-term price movements. Swing trading aims to capture price swings over several days or weeks, while long-term investing focuses on holding assets for extended periods, often years, to benefit from long-term growth.

Each trading strategy has its advantages and disadvantages, and the choice of strategy depends on individual preferences, risk tolerance, and market conditions. Successful traders often combine multiple strategies and adapt their approach based on market trends and personal experiences.

9

Chapter 9: Risk Management and Trading Psychology

Effective risk management and a strong understanding of trading psychology are crucial components of successful cryptocurrency trading. The volatile nature of the crypto market can lead to significant gains, but it also poses substantial risks. Implementing risk management techniques and maintaining a disciplined mindset can help traders navigate these challenges.

One of the key principles of risk management is diversification. By spreading investments across multiple cryptocurrencies, traders can reduce the impact of any single asset's poor performance on their overall portfolio. Diversification helps mitigate risk and provides exposure to various market opportunities.

Position sizing is another critical aspect of risk management. It involves determining the appropriate amount of capital to allocate to each trade based on the trader's risk tolerance and the specific trade's potential. Setting a maximum percentage of capital to risk on any single trade can help prevent significant losses and protect the overall portfolio.

Setting stop-loss and take-profit levels is essential for managing risk and securing profits. These predefined price levels ensure that trades are automatically executed when the market reaches a certain point, helping traders avoid emotional decision-making and maintain discipline.

Trading psychology plays a significant role in a trader's success. Emotions such as fear, greed, and overconfidence can lead to impulsive decisions and negatively impact trading performance. Developing a strong mindset and maintaining discipline are crucial for managing these emotions. Keeping a trading journal, setting realistic goals, and adhering to a well-defined trading plan can help traders stay focused and make rational decisions.

10

Chapter 10: Regulatory Landscape and Compliance

The regulatory landscape for cryptocurrency exchanges is continually evolving. Governments and regulatory bodies worldwide are working to establish frameworks that protect investors, ensure market integrity, and prevent illicit activities such as money laundering and fraud. Understanding the regulatory environment and ensuring compliance is essential for both exchanges and traders.

In many countries, cryptocurrency exchanges are required to implement Know Your Customer (KYC) and Anti-Money Laundering (AML) procedures. KYC involves verifying the identity of users to prevent fraud and ensure compliance with legal requirements. AML measures aim to detect and prevent money laundering activities by monitoring transactions and reporting suspicious activities.

Exchanges must also comply with securities regulations, which can vary significantly between jurisdictions. In some cases, certain cryptocurrencies may be classified as securities, subjecting them to additional regulatory requirements. Understanding these classifications and ensuring compliance is crucial for exchanges to operate legally and avoid penalties.

The evolving regulatory landscape has led to the emergence of self-regulatory organizations (SROs) within the cryptocurrency industry. These organizations aim to establish best practices and standards for exchanges and other market participants. By adhering to these standards, exchanges can demonstrate their commitment to transparency, security, and investor protection.

For traders, staying informed about regulatory developments is essential. Regulations can impact the availability and legality of certain cryptocurrencies and exchanges, as well as the tax implications of trading activities. By understanding the regulatory environment and ensuring compliance, traders can protect their investments and avoid legal issues.

11

Chapter 11: Security Best Practices

Security is a top priority for both cryptocurrency exchanges and traders. The decentralized and digital nature of cryptocurrencies makes them attractive targets for hackers and cybercriminals. Implementing robust security measures can help protect digital assets and ensure a safe trading experience.

For exchanges, security measures include using advanced encryption protocols, multi-factor authentication, and cold storage solutions. Cold storage involves storing cryptocurrencies offline, away from potential cyber threats. Regular security audits and vulnerability assessments can help identify and address potential weaknesses in the exchange's systems.

Traders also play a crucial role in maintaining security. Using strong, unique passwords for exchange accounts and enabling two-factor authentication (2FA) are essential steps. 2FA provides an additional layer of security by requiring a second form of verification, such as a code sent to a mobile device, whenever logging in or making transactions.

Securing personal devices is equally important. Keeping software and antivirus programs up to date, avoiding public Wi-Fi for trading activities, and using hardware wallets for storing cryptocurrencies can help prevent unauthorized access and protect digital assets.

Phishing attacks are a common threat in the cryptocurrency space. These attacks involve fraudulent attempts to obtain sensitive information, such as login credentials and private keys, by masquerading as a legitimate entity. Being vigilant and verifying the authenticity of emails, websites, and communications can help traders avoid falling victim to phishing scams.

By implementing these security best practices, both exchanges and traders can reduce the risk of cyberattacks and protect their digital assets.

12

Chapter 12: The Future of Crypto Exchanges

The future of cryptocurrency exchanges holds exciting possibilities as the industry continues to evolve and mature. Advancements in technology, regulatory developments, and increasing adoption of cryptocurrencies are shaping the landscape of crypto exchanges.

One of the key trends is the rise of decentralized finance (DeFi) platforms. DeFi aims to recreate traditional financial systems using blockchain technology, offering services such as lending, borrowing, and trading without intermediaries. Decentralized exchanges (DEXs) play a central role in the DeFi ecosystem, providing users with greater control over their funds and transactions.

Interoperability between different blockchains is another area of focus. Projects like Polkadot and Cosmos are working to create interconnected networks of blockchains, enabling seamless communication and exchange of assets across different platforms. This development could enhance the liquidity and functionality of cryptocurrency exchanges, making them more efficient and versatile.

Regulatory clarity is also expected to improve as governments and regulatory bodies establish comprehensive frameworks for the cryptocurrency industry. Clear regulations can provide greater certainty for exchanges and investors, fostering trust and encouraging broader adoption of digital assets.

The integration of artificial intelligence (AI) and machine learning (ML) technologies is set to revolutionize crypto exchanges. These technologies can enhance trading algorithms, improve security measures, and provide personalized user experiences. AI and ML can also help detect and prevent fraudulent activities, ensuring a safer and more efficient trading environment.

As the industry continues to grow, the role of education and awareness becomes increasingly important. Exchanges and platforms are likely to invest in educational resources and tools to help users understand the complexities of cryptocurrency trading and navigate the market effectively.

The future of crypto exchanges is undoubtedly dynamic and full of potential. By staying informed and adapting to emerging trends and technologies, both exchanges and traders can seize new opportunities and thrive in the ever-evolving world of cryptocurrency.

www.ingramcontent.com/pod-product-compliance
Lightning Source LLC
LaVergne TN
LVHW020742090526
838202LV00057BA/6197